KIDS' TRAVEL GUIDE
UNITED KINGDOM

Author: Sara-Jane Williams

Editor: Carma Graber

Graphic designer: Francesca Guido

Published by FlyingKids Limited

Visit us @ **www.theflyingkids.com**

Contact us: **leonardo@theflyingkids.com**

ISBN: 978-1-910994-09-2

Acknowledgments
Key: t=top; b=bottom; l=left; r=right, c=center; m=main image; bg=background
All images are from ShutterStock or public domain except those mentioned.
Attributions: 25mtl-By Joel Rouse/ Ministry of Defence [see page for license], via Wikimedia Commons; 25mcr-By Ben from London, United Kingdom (Hello Great Britain) [CC BY-SA 2.0 (http://creativecommons.org/licenses/by-sa/2.0)], via Wikimedia Commons; 34mcr-By Luis Miguel Bugallo Sánchez (Lmbuga Commons)(Lmbuga Galipedia) Publicada por/Published by: Luis Miguel Bugallo Sánchez (Own work) [GFDL (http://www.gnu.org/copyleft/fdl.html) or CC-BY-SA-3.0 (http://creativecommons.org/licenses/by-sa/3.0/)], via Wikimedia Commons.

Table of Contents

Dear Parents,

If you bought this book, you're probably planning a **family trip** with your kids. You are spending a lot of time and money in the hopes that this family vacation will be **pleasant** and **fun**. You would like your children **to learn** a little about the country you visit—its **geography**, **history**, unique **culture**, **traditions**, and more. And you hope they will always remember the trip as a very **special experience**.

The reality is often quite different. Parents find themselves frustrated as they **struggle to convince** their kids to join a tour or visit a landmark, while the kids just want to stay in and watch TV. On the road, the children are glued to their mobile devices instead of enjoying the new sights and scenery—or they complain and constantly ask, **"When are we going to get there?"** Many parents are disappointed after they return home and discover that their kids don't remember much about the trip and the new things they learned.

That's exactly why *Kids' Travel Guide—UK* was created.

With *Kids' Travel Guide—UK*, young children become **researchers** and **active participants** in the trip. They learn fun facts about history and culture; they play games and take quizzes. This helps kids—and parents—**enjoy the trip a lot more!**

How does it work?

A family trip is fun. But **difficulties** can arise when children are not in their **natural environment**.

Kids' Travel Guide—UK takes this into account and supports children as they **get ready** for the trip, **visit** new places, **learn** new things, and finally, **return** home.

The *Kids' Travel Guide—UK* does this by helping children to **prepare for the trip** and know what to expect. During the trip, kids will read **relevant facts** about the United Kingdom and get advice on how to adapt to new situations. *Kids' Travel Guide—UK* includes **puzzles**, **tasks** to complete, useful **tips**, and other **recommendations** along the way. All of this encourages children to experiment, explore, and be more involved in the family's activities—as well as to learn new information and make memories throughout the trip. In addition, kids are asked to **document** and write about their experiences during the trip, so that when you return home, they will have a **memoir** that will be fun to look at and reread **again and again**.

Kids' Travel Guide—UK offers general information about the **UK**, so it is useful **regardless** of the city or part of the country you plan to visit. It includes basic geography; flags, symbols, and coins; basic history; and colorful facts about culture and customs in the United Kingdom.

READY FOR A NEW EXPERIENCE?

Have a nice trip and have fun!

If you are reading this book, it means you are lucky—
you are going to the **United Kingdom**!

You may have noticed that your parents are getting ready for the journey.
They have bought travel guides, looked for information on the Internet,
and printed pages of information. They are talking to friends and people
who have already visited the UK in order to learn about it and know what
to do, where to go, and when ...

But this book is not just another guidebook for your parents.
This book is for you only—the young traveler.

First and foremost, meet Leonardo, your
very own personal guide on this trip.
Leonardo has visited many places
around the world. (Guess
how he got there?)

He will be with you throughout
the book and the trip. Leonardo
will tell you all about the places you will
visit—it is always good to learn a little bit
about the city and its history beforehand.
Leonardo will provide many ideas, quizzes, tips,
and other surprises. He will be with you while you are packing
and leaving home, and he will stay in the hotel with you (don't worry, it
does not cost more money)!
And he will see the sights with you until you return home.

HAVE FUN!

THE BEGINNING!

GOING TO THE UNITED KINGDOM

How did you get to the UK?

By plane / ship / car / other ________________

We will stay in the UK for ______ days.

Is this your first visit ? ________________

Where will you sleep? In a hotel / in a campsite / in a motel / in an apartment / with family / in a guesthouse / other________________

What places are you planning to visit?
____
____
____

What special activities are you planning to do?
____
____
____

Are you excited about the trip?

This is an excitement indicator. Ask your family members how excited they are (from "not at all" up to "very, very much"), and mark each of their answers on the indicator. Leonardo has already marked the level of his excitement ...

Leonardo
very very much!
not at all

Who is traveling?

Write down the names of family members traveling with you and their answers to the questions.

Name: _______________

Age: _______________

Has he or she visited the UK before? yes / no

What is the most exciting thing about your upcoming trip?

____
____
____

Name: _______________

Age: _______________

Has he or she visited the UK before? yes / no

What is the most exciting thing about your upcoming trip?

____
____
____

Name: _______________

Age: _______________

Has he or she visited the UK before? yes / no

What is the most exciting thing about your upcoming trip?

____
____
____

Name: _______________

Age: _______________

Has he or she visited the UK before? yes / no

What is the most exciting thing about your upcoming trip?

____
____
____

Name: _______________

Age: _______________

Has he or she visited the UK before? yes / no

What is the most exciting thing about your upcoming trip?

____
____
____

Preparations at home – do not forget ...!

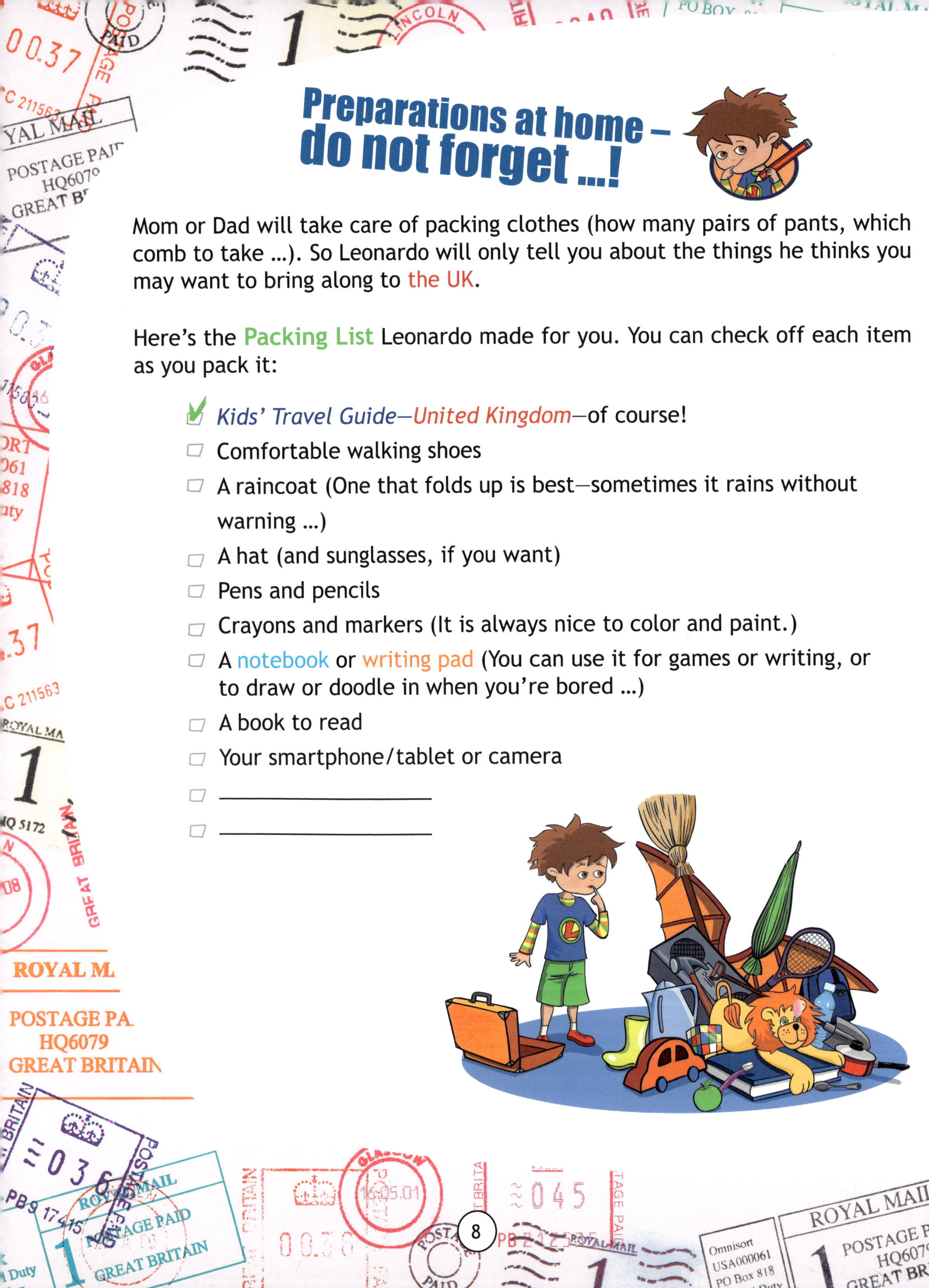

Mom or Dad will take care of packing clothes (how many pairs of pants, which comb to take ...). So Leonardo will only tell you about the things he thinks you may want to bring along to the UK.

Here's the **Packing List** Leonardo made for you. You can check off each item as you pack it:

- ✅ *Kids' Travel Guide—United Kingdom*—of course!
- ☐ Comfortable walking shoes
- ☐ A raincoat (One that folds up is best—sometimes it rains without warning ...)
- ☐ A hat (and sunglasses, if you want)
- ☐ Pens and pencils
- ☐ Crayons and markers (It is always nice to color and paint.)
- ☐ A notebook or writing pad (You can use it for games or writing, or to draw or doodle in when you're bored ...)
- ☐ A book to read
- ☐ Your smartphone/tablet or camera
- ☐ ________________________
- ☐ ________________________

TIPS!

Pack your things in a small bag (or **backpack**). You may also want to take these things:

☐ **Snacks**, **fruit**, **candy**, and **chewing gum**. If you are flying, it can help a lot during takeoff and landing, when there's pressure in your ears.

☐ Games you can play while sitting down: **electronic games**, **booklets** of **crossword puzzles**, connect-the-numbers (or connect-the-dots), etc.

Now let's see if you can find 12 items you should take on a trip in this word search puzzle:

☐ Leonardo
☐ walking shoes
☐ hat
☐ raincoat
☐ crayons
☐ book
☐ pencil
☐ camera
☐ snacks
☐ fruit
☐ patience
☐ good mood

P	A	T	I	E	N	C	E	A	W	F	G
E	L	R	T	S	G	Y	J	W	A	T	O
Q	E	Y	U	Y	K	Z	K	M	L	W	O
H	O	S	N	A	S	N	Y	S	K	G	D
A	N	R	Z	C	P	E	N	C	I	L	M
C	A	M	E	R	A	A	W	G	N	E	O
R	R	A	I	N	C	O	A	T	G	Q	O
Y	D	S	G	I	R	K	Z	K	S	H	D
S	O	A	C	O	A	E	T	K	H	A	T
F	R	U	I	T	Y	Q	O	V	O	D	A
B	O	O	K	F	O	H	Z	K	E	R	T
T	K	Z	K	A	N	S	I	E	S	Y	U
O	V	I	E	S	S	N	A	C	K	S	P

WELCOME TO THE UNITED KINGDOM!

The United Kingdom, or "the **UK**"
for short, is made up of four different countries:
England
Scotland
Wales
Northern Ireland
The UK also includes many **smaller islands around its coast**. It is located in the northwestern part of **Europe**.

The UK has more than 17,000 kilometers (10,560 miles) of coastline—and plenty of pretty **beaches**! 😮 You'll also find beautiful **mountains** and **forests**, rolling **fields**, sparkling **lakes**, rushing **rivers**, exciting **cities**, cute **villages**, lots of **churches**, many **old castles** and **historical spots**, great **shopping**, and loads of things to see and do.

More than **67 million** people live in the UK. And more than **28 million** people visit it every year! 😮 It is the **11th** biggest country in Europe, and it's a popular tourist spot.

Leonardo can't wait to tell you all about this great country. Let's get started …

How many words can you make from "the United Kingdom"? For example: "tent"

____
____
____
____

Did you know?
The full name of the UK is the United Kingdom of Great Britain and Northern Ireland. Great Britain is the main island, which is made up of England, Scotland, and Wales.

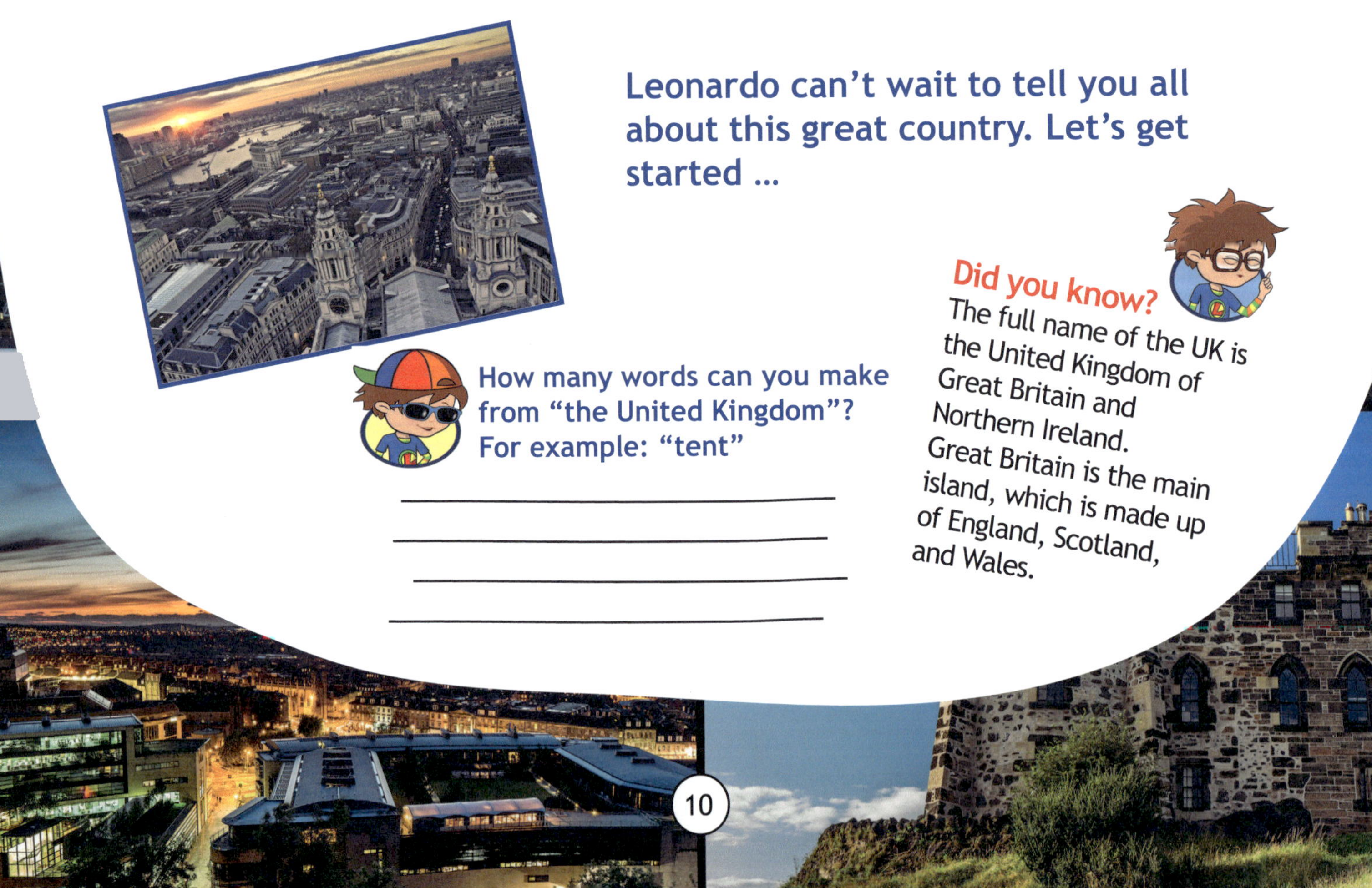

More juicy UK info!

Each country in the UK has its own special feel and traditions—and they each offer something different! They all have their own **flags** and special **saints**. And you may hear **other languages** being spoken along with English!

Leonardo wants to tell you a few things that are special about each country:

England

England is the home of the UK's capital city—London—and it's also very famous for football. The rose is a symbol of England, and Saint George is the special saint. The national tree is the oak tree, a symbol of strength and power. A famous person from English folklore was Robin Hood!

Scotland

Scotland is very famous for kilts and bagpipes. Kilts are similar to skirts, and are worn by both women and men! Bagpipes are musical instruments that people blow into to make a very unusual sound. Traditionally, different family groups in Scottish society were called clans. Clans could be identified by their tartans (a woven cloth that has a special pattern of checks, lines, and colors for each clan).

The thistle plant is the symbol and national flower of Scotland. The special saint is Saint Andrew.

Wales

Wales is a land of dragons and castles! Many famous legends and myths come from Wales. Because of its rich countryside and successful farming, many people think of sheep when they think of Wales! The daffodil and leek are the country's national symbols, and the special saint is Saint David. You'll find the UK's smallest house in Wales!

Northern Ireland

Northern Ireland has not had its own national flag since 1973, but the flag with the red hand is still used unofficially. People often think of the shamrock—a three-leaved clover—when they think about Northern Ireland. The country is also famous for small people called leprechauns! Leprechauns are said to hide a pot of gold at the end of a rainbow. Saint Patrick is the special saint of Northern Ireland.

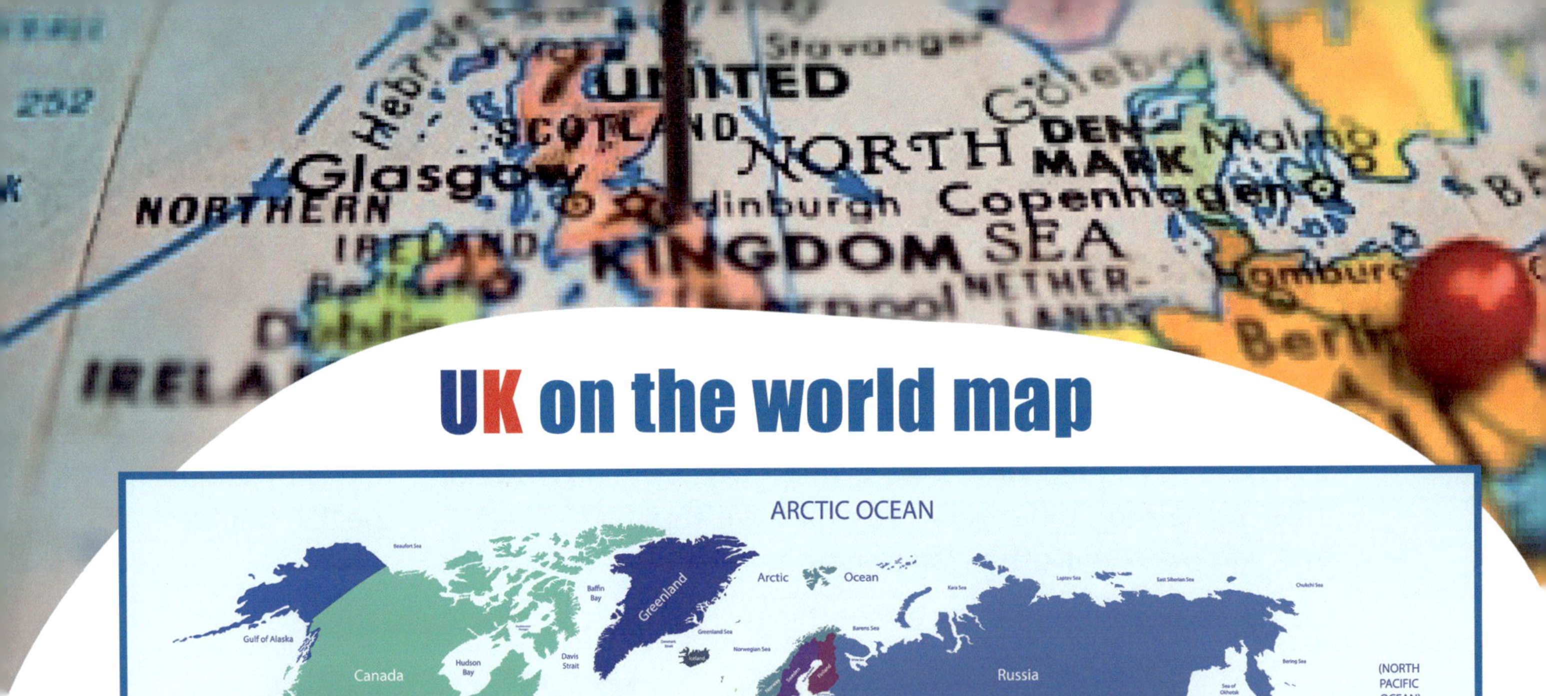

UK on the world map

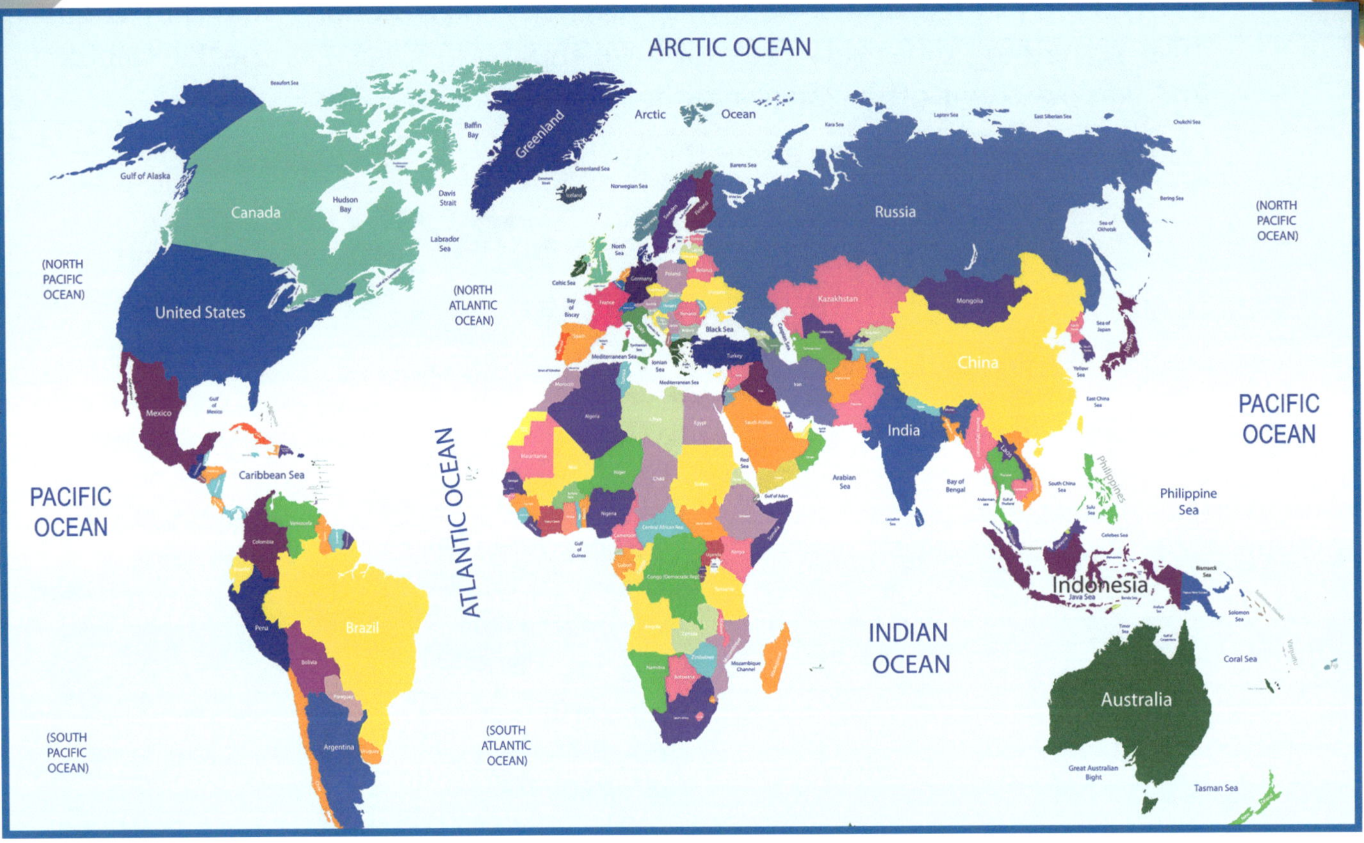

Where is the UK?

This is a map of the world. Can you help Leonardo find the UK? Mark the UK's borders. Find your home country on the map and mark its borders too.

Quizzes!

What **continent** is the UK on? ______________________

How many **countries** make up the UK? ______________________

Answers: Europe; 4 countries

What is a compass rose?

The compass rose is a drawing that shows the directions: North-South-East-West. North is always at the top of the map, and from that you can find the other directions. When you need to get to a place, you can use a compass. A compass rose is drawn on the face of the compass, and the needle always points North. This helps you to navigate and figure out what direction to go—so you can get from one place to another.

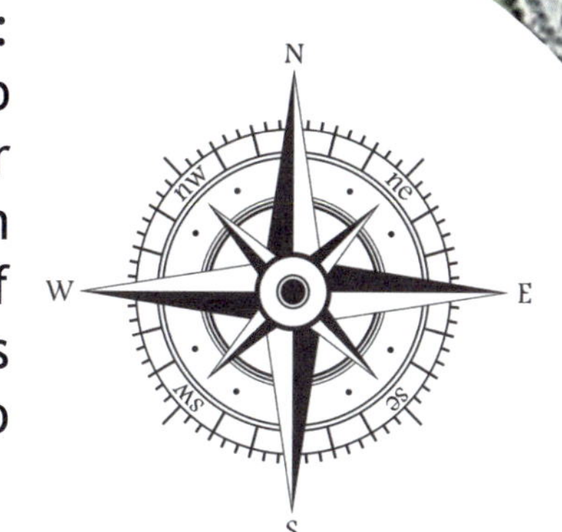

Have you ever used a compass? YES / NO

Write down the three missing directions in the blank squares:

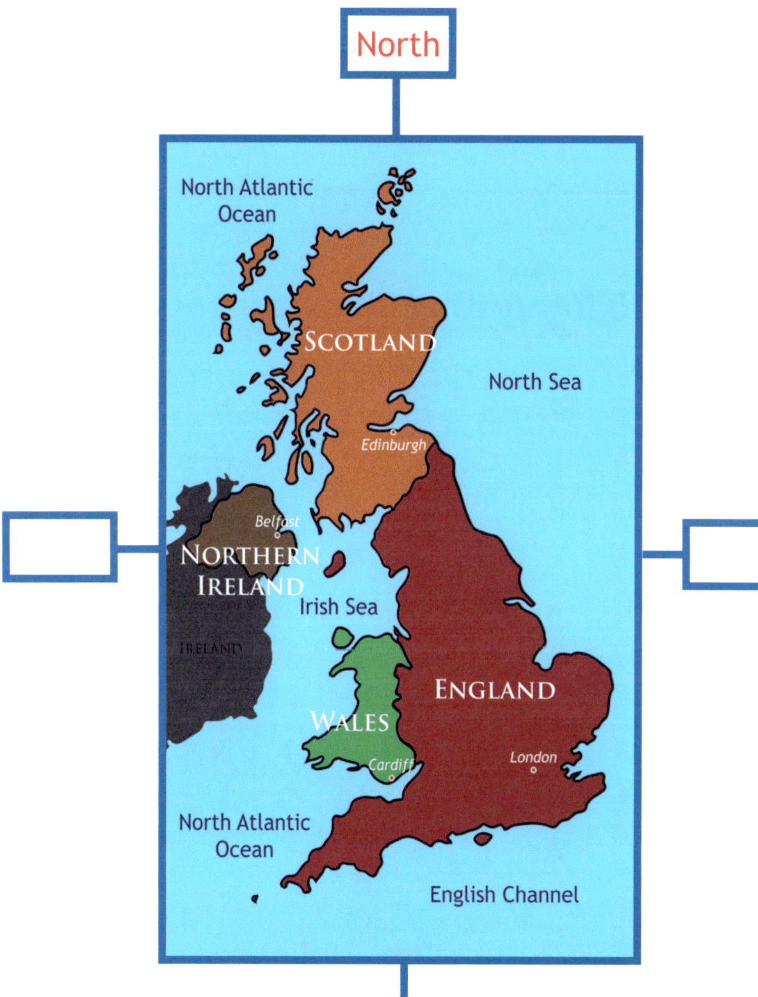

Can you help Leonardo with these directions?

1. What is to the north of England?

____

2. What is to the south of Northern Ireland?

____

3. What is to the east of Wales?

____

4. What sea is to the south of England?

____

5. What sea is to the east of Scotland?

____

Borders—
the lines between neighbors

Did you know?

Borders were invented to show the difference between different countries. A border is a line that marks the end of one country's land and the start of another country's land. There are many kinds of borders: Rivers and mountain ranges can be natural borders. Sometimes fences and gates are built to mark a border.
Countries sometimes end at seas, but many also have islands in the ocean.

There can also be internal borders—for example, between states, regions, counties, and provinces.

There is only one country in the UK that has a land border with two other countries. Do you know what it is? _______________________________________

Help Leonardo find these 10 interesting UK cities:

- ☐ London
- ☐ Belfast
- ☐ Cardiff
- ☐ Swansea
- ☐ Edinburgh
- ☐ Glasgow
- ☐ Birmingham
- ☐ Manchester
- ☐ Liverpool
- ☐ York

L	R	E	T	S	E	H	C	N	A	M
I	O	A	L	C	I	H	A	U	H	A
S	Y	O	K	S	P	Y	R	O	G	H
W	N	W	P	D	O	R	D	C	R	G
A	A	O	X	R	M	N	I	H	U	N
N	I	G	K	E	E	E	F	G	B	I
S	B	S	Z	L	G	V	F	A	N	M
E	E	A	A	N	C	D	I	N	I	R
A	I	L	N	O	D	N	O	L	D	I
U	R	G	A	T	S	A	F	L	E	B

Each country within the UK has its own capital city—although London is the overall capital of the whole United Kingdom.

What is the capital city of your country? _______________________________________

Capital city—London

London is the capital of the UK, and it's also the capital of England. It is the UK's biggest city. It's located in the south of England. London's nickname is "The Smoke." This nickname comes from the days when there was a lot of pollution in the city, so the air was smoky and smoggy!

Did you know?
London was named by the early Romans—they called the city *Londinium*.

Things to do in London

There are so many things to see and do in London! You and your family can visit the official home of the Queen at **Buckingham Palace** and watch the **Changing of the Guard ceremony**. **The Tower of London** is home to the glittering **Crown Jewels** and to big black birds called ravens. You'll see its traditional guards, called **Beefeaters**.

Ride the **London Eye** for amazing views, walk across the famous **Tower Bridge**, be impressed by the huge and beautiful **Westminster Abbey** and **St Paul's Cathedral**, go underground at the **London Dungeons**, see the old and grand **Houses of Parliament**, enjoy **great shopping**, visit the **zoo, parks, and museums** … and more!'

Did you know?
Legend says that there must always be at least six ravens at the Tower of London ... or it will fall down!

Can you draw a circle around London?

Castles and witches!
Edinburgh—the Scottish capital

Edinburgh is the **capital** of Scotland. It is the second biggest city in Scotland—and the seventh biggest in the UK. After London, it's the most popular city in the UK for tourists.

Here are Leonardo's favorite things in Edinburgh!

Edinburgh Castle

You'll see it sitting high up on a hill overlooking the rest of the city. Exploring the castle's many nooks and crannies is lots of fun! The castle is home to the Scottish Crown Jewels, known as the Honours, and some interesting old guns.

The Cadies and Witchery Tour

This is a fun-filled and spooky look at the old part of the city. Guides in wonderful costumes tell tales about witches, ghosts, and mysteries!

Holyrood Palace

This is Queen Elizabeth's official home in Scotland. It is a very grand building with beautiful rooms inside. You can see displays in the gallery that change throughout the year, and the gardens are very pretty.

Edinburgh has many museums, churches, play areas, parks, and shops to see too.

Help Leonardo find Edinburgh on the map and draw a circle around it.

Did you know?
Edinburgh's nickname is Auld Reekie. This means "Old Smoky" in English. Just like London, it got its nickname because the air was so smoky from homes heated with coal fires and the factories.

Time travel to the future and the past ...
Cardiff—the Welsh capital

Cardiff is on the coast of South Wales, and it is the capital city of Wales. It was historically an industrial city, but Cardiff has been through many changes over the years ... There are now lots of modern things, and tons of things for you and your family to see and do!

Did you know?
There are five outstanding castles around Cardiff—perfect for exploring and imagining the past!

Leonardo wants to tell you about these great things to do in Cardiff:

Cardiff Castle is a 2,000-year-old castle and Roman fortress. It has huge gardens and lots of beautiful art. Llandaff Cathedral is one of the oldest religious buildings in all of Europe!

Have you ever wanted to travel through time or meet a Dalek? Cardiff is the home of the famous TV series Doctor Who — you might even spot some filming locations around the city! To step back in time, visit the open-air Museum of Welsh Life, where old houses and shops show how people once lived. Cardiff also has great beaches!

Did you know?
Cardiff has the most park space per person of all the UK's cities. This means there are plenty of places for you to run and play!

Help Leonardo write the names of these famous Cardiff sights:

D_ _t_ r W_o E_ _ _ ri_ _ _e
C_ _ _ i_ _ C_ s_ _ _
L_ an_ _f_ C_ _ _e_ _a_

Can you spot Cardiff on the map? Put a star next to it.

Dinosaurs, mummies, caves, and more ...
Belfast—the Northern Irish capital

Belfast is both the capital city and the biggest city of Northern Ireland.

It was a very dangerous city in the past, with lots of fighting and violence between Northern Ireland and the Republic of Ireland. These times were known as "The Troubles."

Luckily, today, Belfast is a vibrant, welcoming city known for its peace and creativity.

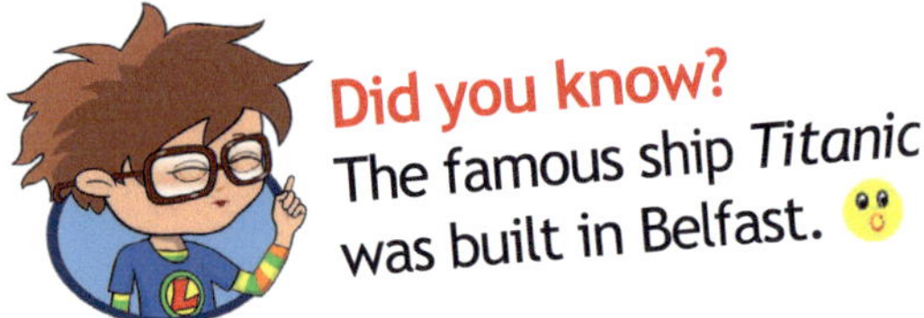

Did you know?
The famous ship *Titanic* was built in Belfast.

But what can you DO in Belfast?—LOTS!
These are some top things that Leonardo recommends:

Belfast Castle and Cave Hill
The castle itself is fairly new (compared to other castles)—it only dates back to 1870! It is more like a big and grand house. The nearby caves are incredibly cool and great for exploring!

Belfast Zoo
Do you love animals? Then Belfast Zoo will provide a fun day for you and your family! It has a splendid lake and lots of animals!

Ulster Museum
Have you ever wanted to get up close and personal with dinosaurs? Or learn more about ancient Egyptian mummies? These are just two things you can do at this fab museum!

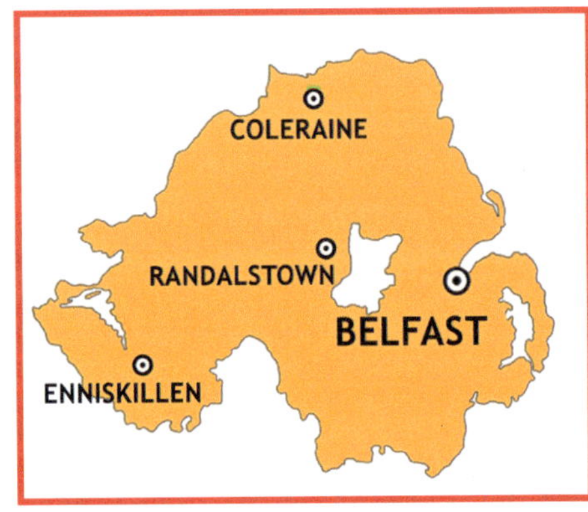

Help Leonardo by drawing a **star** next to Belfast on the map.

Flag and symbols

This is the flag of the UK. It was created in 1801.

As you can see, the flag has three colors—red, white, and blue. There's a special flag for each saint, and the UK flag combines the flags of the patron saints of England, Scotland, and Ireland.

The UK flag is usually called the **Union Jack**.

Some other countries (and states/provinces) use the Union Jack on their flags too. This is because in the past they were part of the **British Empire**—and were ruled by Britain.

Did you know?
Wales is not represented in the UK's flag. That's because when the flag was designed, Wales wasn't yet part of the UK.

What two animals can you see in the Coat of Arms?

_______________________ _______________________

Answers: Lion and Unicorn

This is the **Royal Coat of Arms of the UK**.

Animal symbols of the UK are the **lion** and the **bulldog**.

Did you know?
The motto at the bottom of the Coat of Arms is not written in English! It is actually written in French! It means *"God and my right."*

Does your country have any special symbols?

____

What animal is on the Coat of Arms and is also a symbol of the UK? _______________________

Answer: Lion

How to buy things in the UK

The type of money that a country uses is called its currency. The UK's currency is the **pound sterling**—or just the "pound."

There are 100 pennies (called pence) in a pound. (Pence is often shortened to "p".)

Coins come in amounts of 1p, 2p, 5p, 10p, 20p, and 50p. There are also 1-pound and 2-pound coins. Notes (or bills) come in the values of 5, 10, 20, and 50 pounds.

Since 2023, all new banknotes and coins feature **King Charles III**. But many with Queen Elizabeth II's image are still in use.

Some of the coins were made so that you could fit together the 50p, 20p, 10p, 5p, 2p, and 1p coins to create a picture of a shield! The 1-pound coin shows the full shield.

Did you know?
Every coin shows the year it was produced.
Can you find a coin that was made in the year you were born?

Did you know?
A shape with seven sides is called a heptagon.

Quizzes!

A. What is the smallest value of coin? _______________

B. What is the biggest value of coin? _______________

C. What is the biggest value of note? _______________

D. What is the smallest value of note? _______________

E. How many sides does a 50p coin have? _______________

F. Whose picture is on all notes and coins? _______________

G. What color is the 20-pound note? _______________

Leonardo drew a pound symbol. Can you copy him?

£

Answers: A- 1 pence; B- 2 pounds; C- 50 pounds; D- 5 pounds; E- 7; F- The queen; G- Purple

History of England—
lots of battles and wars!

England has a long and very colorful history! The country has been captured and occupied by many different groups over time. And, in turn, England has conquered plenty of other countries too!

Leonardo will tell you about some of the main events in this fascinating history:

Invasions

The Romans invaded England as far back as 55 BC! They ruled England for 400 years, and there are still many Roman ruins all around the country today.

In 1066 AD, France captured England. There was a very famous battle called the Battle of Hastings. France's king then became the King of England!

A deadly disaster!

Between the 1340s and 1350s, a devastating plague killed almost one-third of England's population!

Power hungry

In the 1400s and 1500s, England conquered many other countries, creating a large global empire. England held power in the USA, Australia, New Zealand, Singapore, India ... and other places! England also conquered Wales!

Not-so-friendly neighbors!
(who then became friends ...)

Throughout history, there were many battles between England, Scotland, and Wales.

Then in 1707, England and Scotland joined together under one leadership and became Great Britain. Ireland joined them in 1801, but then left again in 1921.

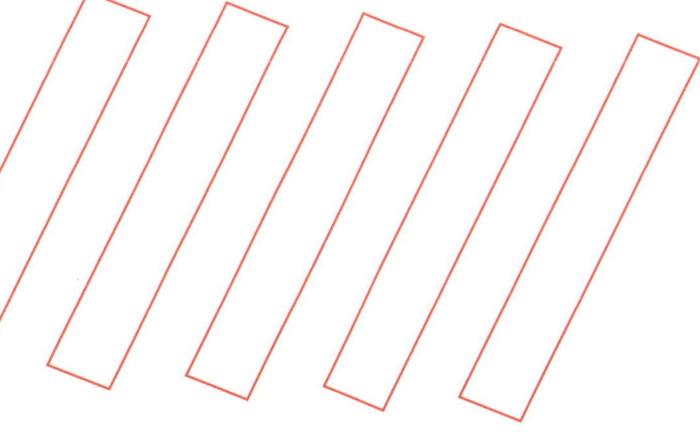

Leonardo is a little bit confused ... Can you help him to put the events of England's long history in order?

History of Scotland—
from the Ice Age to today—clans, kings, and battles

People have lived in Scotland since the end of the Ice Age—that was around 10,000 years ago!

Did you know?
There are many castles in Scotland. These were built to keep invaders out!

Roman invasions

By the first century AD, a lot of what is now Scotland was part of the mighty Roman Empire. But the Romans never conquered Scotland's northern territory. It was called Caledonia, and the Romans called its native people "Picti"—or "painted"—because they painted their bodies!

The Romans built a huge wall—which they named Hadrian's Wall, after their Emperor— to keep the Picti people away. You can still walk along Hadrian's Wall today!

Scots are from ... Ireland?!?!

Later, the land was invaded by Scots people—who came from Ireland!

Kingdoms combined

Several rival kingdoms joined together in the ninth century to create the Kingdom of Scotland. They fought many wars with England!

Unity

In the 1700s, Scotland and England joined together with one parliament, although Scotland kept its own religion and legal system.

Take a picture of a magnificent Scottish castle.

History of Wales—
land of legends, dragons, castles, and fights!

Early humans lived in the land now known as Wales many thousands of years ago. During the Ice Age, large mammoths and reindeer roamed freely.

Let Leonardo take you on an adventure through Wales's exciting history! 

Celts, Druids, and magic!

Around 1000 BC, people called Celts came from other parts of Europe to the area that is now Wales. You can still see many Celtic influences in Wales today. The Celts were led by Druids—a type of priests. They followed a religion based on nature and magic!

Invasions and castles

Wales was invaded many times—by the Romans, the Saxons, the English, and the Normans, to name just a few! Many castles were built across the country to protect the lands from outside invaders. Today, the remains of 600 old castles can be found around the country!

Myths and legends

Have you ever heard of King Arthur and the Knights of the Round Table? Or the magical Kingdom of Camelot? Or Merlin the Wizard? These tales all have roots in Welsh history and legend!

Another popular Welsh legend is the **red dragon** and the white dragon ... Merlin the Wizard said that the white dragon of the Saxons would rule Wales at first, but would then be defeated by the red dragon!

Can you draw Merlin the Wizard and a dragon?

History of Northern Ireland—
troubled times and a country divided

Northern Ireland and the Republic of Ireland were once one united country. Leonardo will tell you more about Ireland's past, and how it eventually split into two:

The English connection

In 1170, the English first took an interest in Ireland's affairs. After the English helped the Irish in a battle, they were **given land** in Ireland as a reward.

At first the English controlled just a small part of the country. But in 1541, the King of England made himself **King of Ireland** too. That led to many **fights**!

In 1801, Ireland was officially joined with England, Scotland, and Wales to create the **Union of Great Britain and Ireland**. But many troubles followed …

Starvation

The Irish potato crop failed for several years in the mid-1800s. This caused a **huge famine** in Ireland, and many people starved to death. It's known as the **Potato Famine**. The English wouldn't help the starving people, and this made the Irish hate the English even more!

Separate countries

In 1948, the Republic of Ireland became an **independent** country. Northern Ireland stayed with the UK. There were troubles, though, until the 1990s.

Quizzes!

1. What reward were the English given in 1170?

A. Bread

B. Gold

C. Land

D. Money

2. A lack of which food caused the big famine?

A. Carrots

B. Fish

C. Burgers

D. Potatoes

Being royal ... about the **Royal Family**

The Royal Family means all the close members of the **king's** large family. The **current monarch is King Charles the Third (King Charles III).**

Can you guess why he is called the Third?

What's in a name?

The Royal Family has had several last names over the years, including Tudor, Stuart, Hanover, and Wessex. These last names are often called Houses. The current Royal Family's last name is Windsor—or the House of Windsor.

Who will be next?

When a king or queen dies or steps down, their oldest child becomes the next king or queen. If the king or queen has no children, there are complicated rules—called the order of succession—that decide who is next in line for the throne.

Did you know?
King Henry the 8th is known for having lots of wives—he had six!

Did you know?
Although the King or Queen may sometimes live in other homes—like Clarence House—**Buckingham Palace** is still the house for big royal events and ceremonies!

Does your country have a king or queen?   Yes / No

Did your country have a royal family in the past?   Yes / No

Would you like to be a royal?
Yes / No / Maybe ...

Here is a beautiful crown for you to color.

Culture and customs

The UK really is a big mixture of many different cultures and customs! All four countries have their own very different ways and traditions.

Many other groups have also chosen to move to the UK over the years, and they brought their own customs with them. The cultures of other European countries have influenced the UK too.

Leonardo will tell you some interesting things about British culture:

☑ The normal greeting is a handshake, although hugs are now very common between friends.

☑ British people are often said to be quite reserved. This means they don't show lots of emotions in public. This can make them seem pretty formal and dull at times! But they're not really!

☑ Many Brits don't like to hold eye contact for long.

☑ Brits are known for drinking lots of tea!

TIP!

Don't assume that everyone you meet is English! People from the other countries in the UK can be quite proud of their roots, and they do not like being called English. It is better to call everyone British.

Look around you ... can you help Leonardo find more customs from the UK?

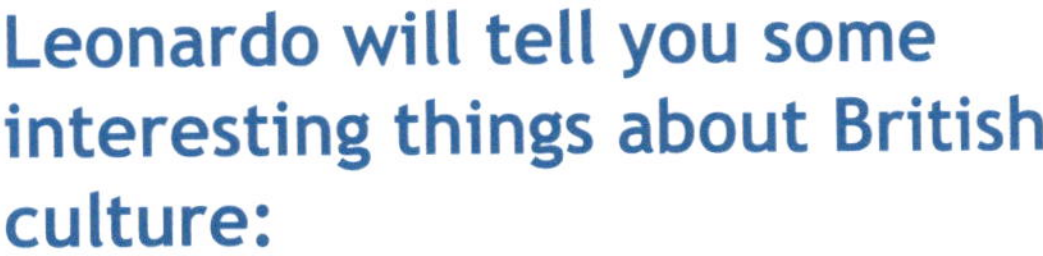

____

____

____

There are lots of superstitions in the UK!
Leonardo will tell you about some of them. (Do you have any of these in your country?)

Breaking a **mirror** brings seven years' bad luck! 😜

Opening an **umbrella** inside is bad luck. So is walking under a **ladder**, spilling **salt**, and putting **new shoes** on a table!

Lucky things include **black cats**, **horseshoes** (but only the right way up!), four-leafed **clovers**, and touching **wood**!

Try to take a picture of a black cat.

Do you know of any other UK superstitions?

____

____

Does your country have any superstitions?

____

Do you know what a **magpie** is? It's a black-and-white bird. In the UK, seeing magpies means different things, depending on how many of them you see. There is even a rhyme to help people remember! *"One for sorrow, Two for joy, Three for a girl, Four for a boy …"*

(This means seeing one magpie is unlucky, but two are lucky. Three magpies mean a baby girl will be born, and four mean a baby boy!)

Eating in the UK

Traditional meals in most parts of the UK were made up of meat, potatoes, and two different kinds of vegetables. Times have changed though, and now you can find food from all over the world in the UK.

There are still several dishes that are special to the UK, and some that are common to each of the different countries within the UK. Even more meals are specialties of different regions in the UK.

Let Leonardo introduce you to some of the UK's wonderful food! 😉

Roast Dinner

The roast dinner is sometimes called the UK's national dish. It is traditionally eaten on a Sunday, so it's also known as a Sunday roast.

It includes roasted meat, different kinds of vegetables, roast potatoes, and gravy. Depending on what meat is served, other items can vary.

Fish and Chips

This popular meal consists of batter-coated fried fish and chips (deep-fried potatoes similar to french fries). Takeaway shops traditionally sold it wrapped up in newspaper!

Some people eat fish and chips with gravy, mushy peas, or curry sauce.

Did you know?

Putting your elbows on the table when you eat is considered quite impolite in the UK!

Haggis

Haggis is a Scottish dish. Traditionally, it is made by stuffing a sheep's stomach with other parts of a sheep—and a mixture of onion, spices, oatmeal, suet, and gravy.

What's your favorite food from the UK?

____

Do you want to try it?
Yes____ No____ Maybe____

Pies, pasties, and puddings

Pies and pasties

Have you tasted a pie in England? Is it different from the pies in your country? English pies and pasties are similar—both contain a different selection of meats and vegetables, surrounded with a pastry crust. Pasties are supposed to be a meal on their own. Pies usually come with chips or mashed potatoes, vegetables, and gravy.

Soda bread

Common in Northern Ireland, soda bread is delicious and fluffy!

Did you know?

A pasty in Northern Ireland is different than a pasty in England. In Northern Ireland, it is similar to a burger.

Cooked breakfast

You might also hear this called a "fry-up" —because most of the items are fried!

A cooked breakfast can contain a combination of many things. Some of the most popular are bacon, sausages, fried eggs or scrambled eggs, fried mushrooms and tomatoes, hash browns, baked beans, fried bread or toast, and black pudding.

Did you know?

Black pudding is actually made from pig's blood!

Have you come across these in the UK? Do you know what they are called?

Draw on the plate what you ate for breakfast this morning.

Answer: Crumpets

Even MORE fabulous food!

Scones

Scones are a very English or Welsh treat. They are like small, heavy, thick cakes, usually served with jam and cream. They are often enjoyed in the afternoon with a pot of tea.

Did you know?
The sandwich was invented in the UK, near London. The Earl of Sandwich was too busy to stop playing a card game, so he asked his staff to bring him some meat between two pieces of bread!

Take a picture of your favorite UK meal.

Help Leonardo find these different foods:

- ☐ Bread
- ☐ Cheese
- ☐ Meat
- ☐ Pie
- ☐ Chicken
- ☐ Fish
- ☐ Chips
- ☐ Potato
- ☐ Apple
- ☐ Scone
- ☐ Peas
- ☐ Pasty

I	E	S	A	E	P	N	R	I	T
E	L	G	D	A	E	R	B	Y	P
N	P	A	S	K	H	M	H	W	O
O	P	M	C	H	E	E	S	E	T
C	A	I	J	W	I	A	I	H	A
S	H	N	E	E	N	T	F	S	T
C	A	P	A	S	T	Y	C	U	O

What's your favorite food from your country?

____

____

____

Language in the UK

English is the most widely spoken language in the UK. It is the first language of many other countries around the world too. And it's one of the most-learned second languages all around the globe.

Did you know?

Many other languages are spoken in the UK besides English! Some people in Wales speak Welsh. In Northern Ireland, people may speak Irish and Ulster Scots. And some people in Scotland speak Scottish Gaelic, which is very similar to Ulster Scots.

Different groups of immigrants over the years have also brought their own languages with them. There are entire UK communities that speak Chinese, Polish, Arabic, Urdu ... and many, many more!

Leonardo can say **hello** in Irish and Welsh! Can you say hello in any other languages? Write in the speech bubbles.

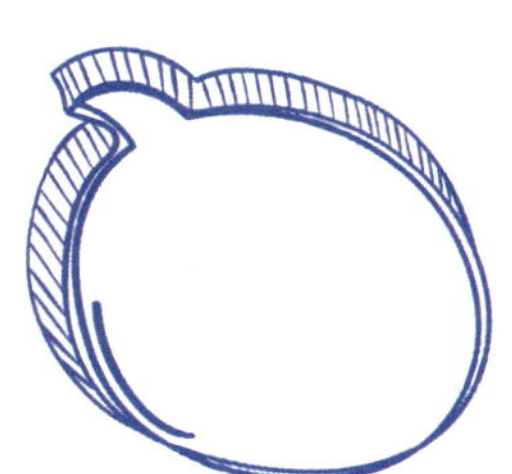

Many influences

The English language has been shaped by many other languages throughout history. It has taken lots of words from other languages too!

Variations

"Accents" are differences in how English is pronounced in different areas. But "dialect" is more than just a different accent. A dialect has words and phrases that are only used in one particular area.

Strange facts about the English language

Sometimes people from different parts of the UK have trouble understanding each other because of their different accents and dialects.

Bap, Batch, Cob, Barm, Muffin, Bridie, Rowie, Stottie, and *Oggie* are all words used in different parts of the UK for the same type of food. Can you guess which food it is?

Answer: B – They are all different words used for bread rolls!

Can you think of any more English idioms?

____

____

____

Interesting idioms

Do you know what an idiom is?

It's a phrase that means something different than the actual words. English is full of fabulous idioms. Leonardo will share some with you:

"It's Raining Cats and Dogs"

Don't worry—there are no cats or dogs about to fall on you! This means it's raining really hard!

"A Piece of Cake"

It you can't see an actual piece of cake, this phrase means that something is very easy to do.

Can you draw a cool picture to show another one of these idioms?

"Hold Your Horses"

Don't panic, nobody REALLY wants you to hold back any horses! This means to wait and be patient.

"Let the Cat Out of the Bag"

There's no cat in a bag really … This means to let a secret slip out by accident.

Fun facts! What's the biggest, fastest, oldest ...?

Everyone's interested in all the strange and unique things that make a place special, right? So let's have a look at some of these interesting things from the UK!

Windsor Castle is the **biggest and oldest** castle in the world that still has people living in it!

Cumberland Pencil Museum is home to the **longest colored pencil** on the planet! It is eight meters (**26** feet) long!

London is the **only city** to have hosted the Olympic Games **three times**!

Scotland is said to be home to a large and mysterious water creature—called the **Loch Ness Monste**r! Each year, a million people visit Loch Ness to try to spot **Nessie**.

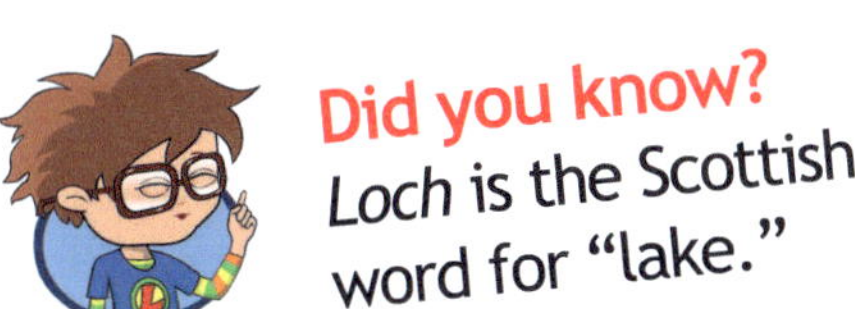

Did you know?
Loch is the Scottish word for "lake."

Can you believe it!? Even MORE fun facts!

No place in the UK is more than 120 km (75 miles) from the sea!

A place in Wales has the **longest name** in Europe, and one of the longest place names in the world: "Llanfairpwllgwyngyllgogerychwyrndrobwllllantysiliogogogoch." Try to say it! 😮

In 2022, Queen Elizabeth II passed away after reigning for 70 years—making her the UK's longest-reigning monarch ever! Her son, King Charles III, took the throne after her.

The world's biggest **prawn cocktail** was made in the UK.

There is a **butterfly** named after the UK's flag—it's called the **Union Jack.** But ... the butterfly comes from Australia!

Bala Lake in Wales is home to a rare type of **fish** called the **gwyniad**. This is thought to be the only place in the world where these fish live.

Can you remember the colors of the Union Jack? Color this butterfly using the flag's colors.

Quizzes!

1. Who was the longest reigning UK monarch?

____

2. What is the Australian butterfly named after?

____

3. What country is Mount Everest in?

____

Answers: 1. Queen Elizabeth II; 2. UK's flag (the Union Jack); 3. Nepal

Lots of sports

Football

The most popular sport in the UK is football, also known as soccer. Many people believe it was actually started in England, although the modern game of football is very different than the early game where people just kicked a ball around!

There are more than 100 teams in the UK's football league, although only the best 20 play in the top league—the Premier League.

Do you know any famous football teams from the UK?

____

____

Do you have a favorite team? _______________________

Help Leonardo to figure out which sports are team sports and which are individual sports (where you play on your own, usually against one other person).

Tennis, Netball, Rugby, Football, Volleyball, Badminton, Cricket, Table Tennis, Hockey, Basketball, Baseball.

Team

Individual

Cricket

Cricket—a bat-and-ball game—is the national sport of the UK. It spread all around the world after its birth in England.

Rugby

Rugby is a rough sport (American football came from rugby). In the past, rugby was mainly played by the upper classes. But today, anyone can play. It is especially popular in Wales. There are two types of rugby—League and Union—and each has different rules.

Other popular sports in the UK include tennis, badminton, swimming, netball, and rowing.

Leonardo loves tennis! What is your favorite sport to play or do?

____

What is your favorite sport to watch?

____

What sports are popular in your country?

____

____

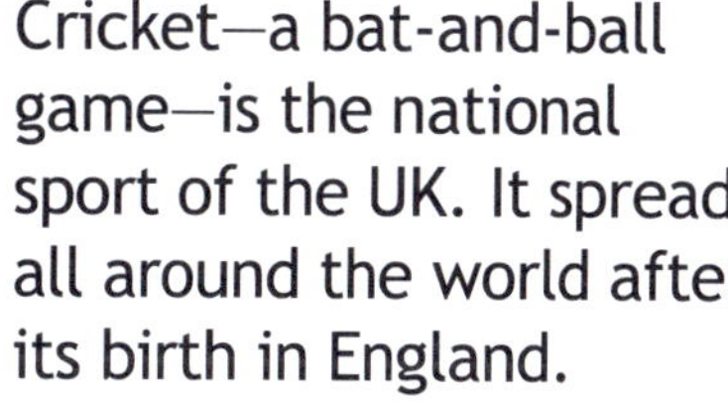

Brainy UK trivia quiz!

1. What **four countries** make up the UK? ______________ , ______________ , ______________ , ______________

2. What is the **UK's capital city**? ______________

3. What is **Edinburgh's nickname**? ______________

4. Where can you find **bagpipes**? ______________

5. What **city** is home to Llandaff Cathedral? ______________

6. What color is the **dragon** on the Welsh flag? ______________

7. What is the capital city of **Northern Ireland**? ______________

8. What will fall down if the **ravens** leave? ______________

9. What is the **nickname** of the UK's flag? ______________

10. What is the **currency** of the UK? ______________

11. Who is shown on all **UK money**? ______________

12. How many types of **rugby** are there? ______________

13. How do people usually **greet** each other? ______________

Answers: 1. England, Scotland, Wales, and Northern Ireland;
2. London; 3. Auld Reekie; 4. Scotland; 5. Cardiff; 6. Red; 7. Belfast;
8. Tower of London; 9. Union Jack; 10. Pound Sterling; 11. The queen;
12. Two; 13. Handshake

More brainy UK trivia quiz!

14. What should you keep off tables at mealtimes? _______________________

15. Where were Scots people originally from? _______________________

16. The rare creatures that live in Bala Lake are a type of what? _______________

17. What black pet is said to be lucky?_______________________

18. What is the King's first name? _______________________

19. What part of the UK suffered from a terrible potato famine? _______________

20. What is a lock? _______________________

21. Complete this idiom: "It's raining _________ and _________ ."

22. Was cricket invented in England, Scotland, Wales or Northern Island? _________
____

23. Who hides pots of gold at the end of the rainbow? _______________________

24. Where is soda bread popular? _______________________

25. What dish is popular? Fish and _________

26. What country's flag is blue with a white cross? _______________________

Answers: 14. Elbows; 15. Ireland; 16. Fish; 17. Cat; 18. Charles;
19. Ireland; 20. Lake; 21. Cats and Dogs;
22. England; 23. Leprechauns; 24. Northern Ireland;
25. Chips; 26. Scotland

Fun Page!

 You already know that one of the UK's national animals is the lion ... so here's a lovely lion for you to color.

Now give it an awesome name! 

My lion is called ________________________

 Can you draw a line to match the balls to their sports?

1. Football

2. Rugby

3. Tennis

4. Basketball

5. Golf

6. Cricket

 A

 B

 C

 D

 E

 F

Answers: 1. E, 2. F, 3. A, 4. C, 5. B, 6. D

Funny money!

If you have 10 pounds and you buy a T-shirt for 5 pounds, a toy for 2 pounds, and a pencil for 50p, how much change will you get back?

____

If you want to buy a key ring for 75p, what coins do you need to use the fewest coins AND give the exact money?

____

Leonardo buys a shirt for 15 pounds, a toy for 5 pounds, a chocolate bar for 1 pound, a bottle of water for 1 pound, and a pencil for 30p. What is his total bill?

____

Answers: 2 pounds and 50 pence; 50p + 20p + 5p, 22 pounds and 30 pence

 How many words can you make from "Buckingham Palace"? For example: "cup":

____

____

____

Break the code!

Use the key below to figure out Leonardo's journal entry about his trip to the UK:

A = &, C = 9, E = X, L = 1, O = J, N = *, P = #, S = 6, T = %

My trip to the U*I%XD KI*GDJM (_ _ _ _ _ _ _ _ _ _ _ _ _ _) was amazing! I went to many great cities ... It is hard to choose a favorite, but I loved 1J*DJ* (_ _ _ _ _ _) and XDI*BURGH (_ _ _ _ _ _ _ _ _) lots.

I saw lots of terrific things too. The 9&6%1X6 (_ _ _ _ _ _ _ _) were incredible—I like to see old places from times gone by. We went to BX1F&6% (_ _ _ _ _ _ _) Zoo and I saw many animals. My favorites were the lions. I really liked the %JWXR of 1J*DJ* (_ _ _ _ _ of _ _ _ _ _ _), and Llandaff 9&%HXDR&1 (_ _ _ _ _ _ _ _ _). I even spent some time relaxing on a pretty BX&9H (_ _ _ _ _ _).

I wish we had seen the QUXX* (_ _ _ _ _) at Buckingham #&1&9X (_ _ _ _ _ _ _)! But we did see people playing B&G#I#X6 (_ _ _ _ _ _ _ _ _) when we went to 69J%1&*D (_ _ _ _ _ _ _ _)—that was cool!

FI6H and 9HI#6 (_ _ _ _ and _ _ _ _ _) is a delicious meal ... scones are nice too. I had a RJ&6% (_ _ _ _ _ _) dinner every Sunday.

I bought lots of presents for my friends at home. Using #JU*D6 (_ _ _ _ _ _ _) is easy when you get the hang of it!

I loved the UK, and I can't wait to go back there again!

Unscramble these famous places and things from the UK:

(City) dfafCri ———————————

(Thing) iLno ———————————

(City) dnoLno ———————————

(Thing) selCta ———————————

(City) bgndhEriu ———————————

(Thing) ncinUro ———————————

(City) flatBse ———————————

(Thing) gHgisa ———————————

Summary of the trip

We had great fun, what a pity it is over ...

Whom did we meet ...

Did you meet tourists from other countries? Yes/No

**If you did meet tourists, where did they come from?
(Name their nationalities):**

____

____

Shopping and souvenirs ...

What did you buy on the trip?

____

____

What did you want to buy, but ended up not buying?

____

____

Experiences

What are the most memorable experiences of the trip?

____

____

____

Rating the trip:
Our favorite things

Grade the most beautiful places and the best experiences of your journey:

First Place

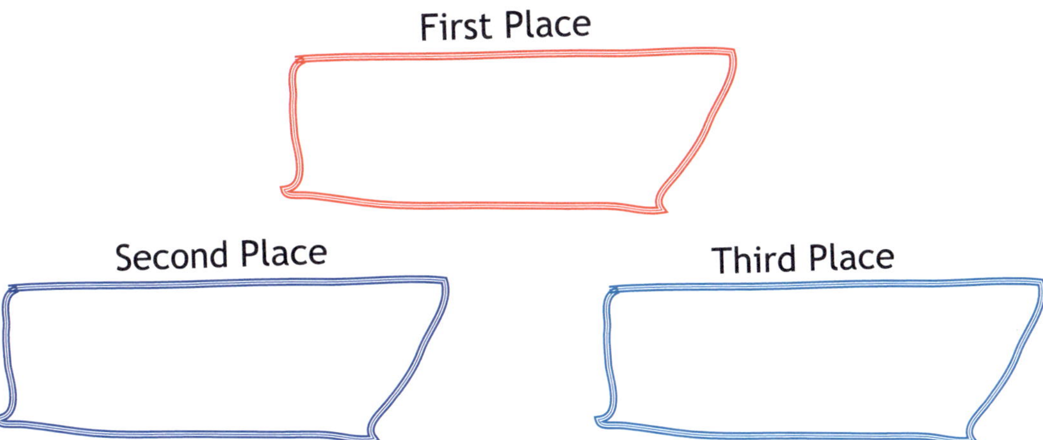

Second Place

Third Place

And now, a difficult task—discuss it with your family and decide ...

What did you enjoy most on the trip?

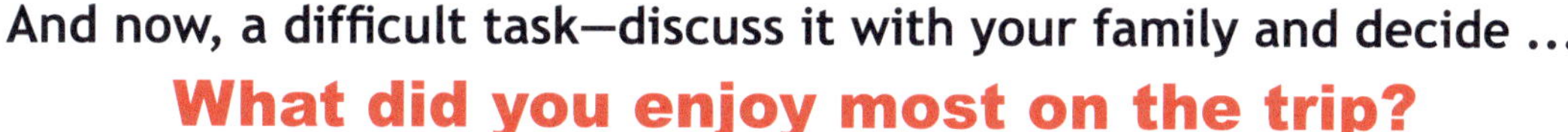

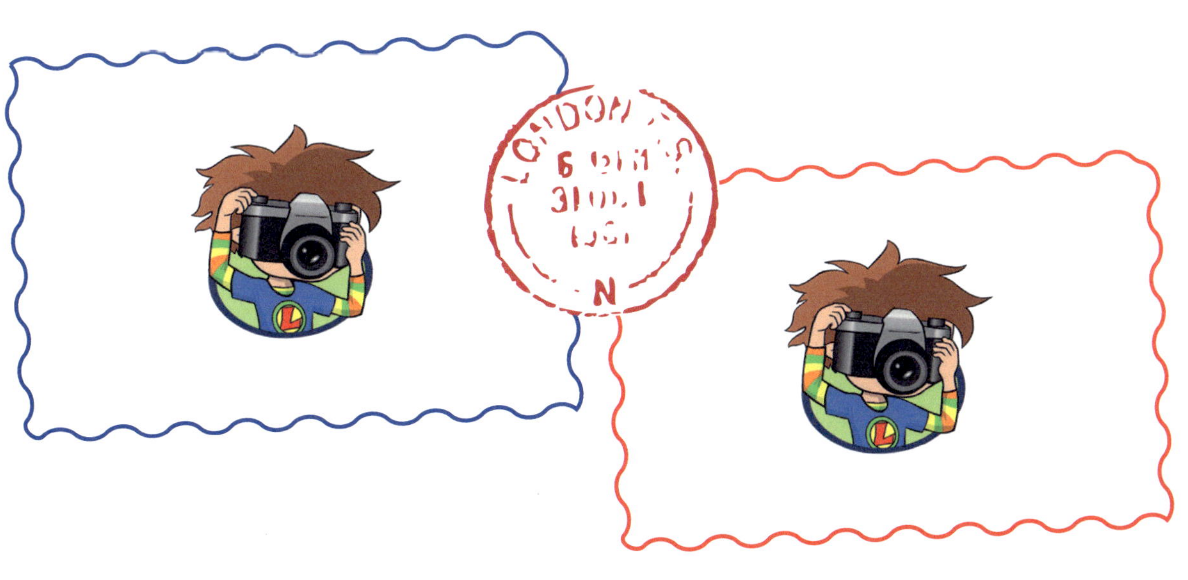

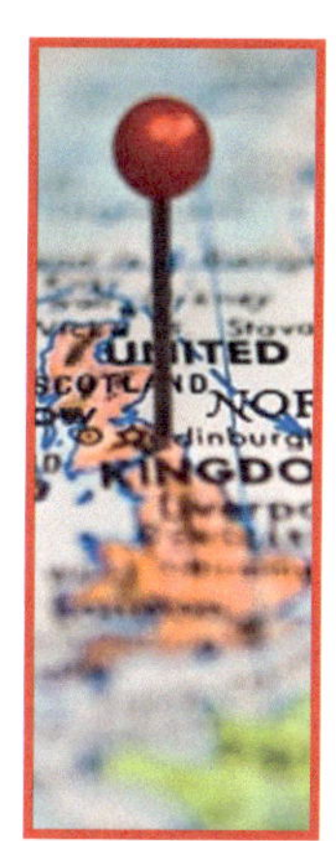

A journal

Date | What did we do?

A journal

ENJOY MORE FUN ADVENTURES WITH LEONARDO AND FlyingKids®

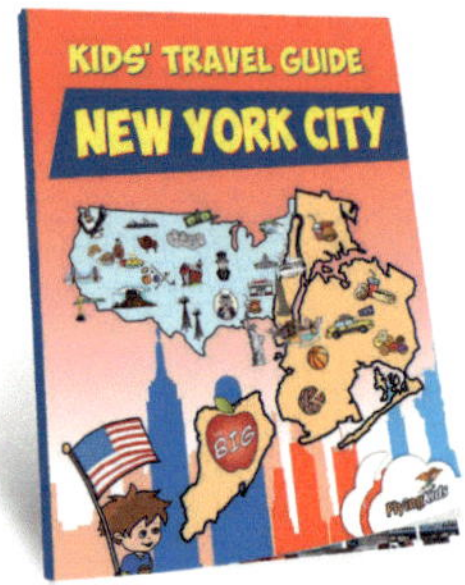

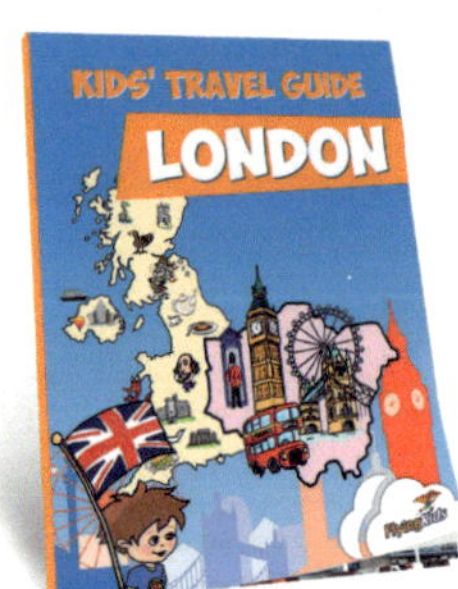

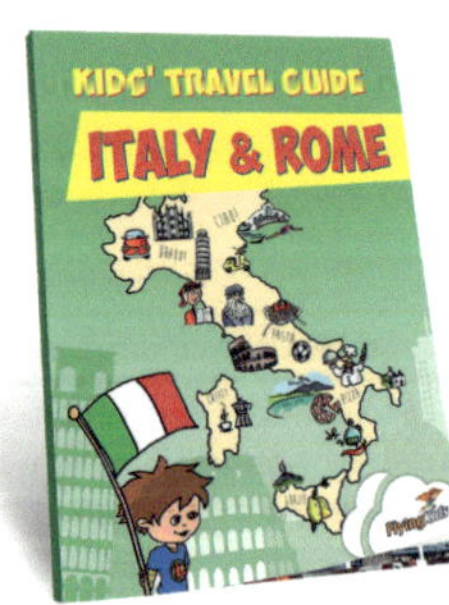

FOR FREE DOWNLOADS OF MORE ACTIVITIES, GO TO
WWW.THEFLYINGKIDS.COM